—FOODS OF—
ITALY

by Christine Velure Roholt

BELLWETHER MEDIA • MINNEAPOLIS, MN

Library of Congress Cataloging-in-Publication Data

VeLure Roholt, Christine, author.
 Foods of Italy / by Christine VeLure Roholt.
    pages cm. -- (Express. Cook with Me)
 Summary: "Information accompanies step-by-step instructions on how to cook Italian food. The text level and subject matter are intended for students in grades 3 through 7"-- Provided by publisher.
 Audience: Age 7-12.
 Audience: Grades 3-7.
 Includes bibliographical references and index.
 ISBN 978-1-62617-119-0 (hardcover : alk. paper)
1. Cooking, Italian--Juvenile literature. 2. Food habits--Italy--Juvenile literature. 3. Italy--Social life and customs--Juvenile literature. I. Title.
 TX723.V415 2014
 641.5945--dc23
                         2014013108

This edition first published in 2015 by Bellwether Media, Inc.

Printed in the United States of America, North Mankato, MN.

Table of Contents

Cooking the Italian Way

Italy is a country with strong regional **traditions**. Different **climates** and landscapes define each area and the food grown there. Because of this **diversity**, there are many styles of cooking in Italy. Some foods, such as pasta, can be found all over. However, each region has its own way of preparing these **staples**. Families and communities pass down recipes through generations. These traditions ensure that Italian **cuisine** stays rich and varied.

The best Italian cuisine is made simply. Most recipes use just a few ingredients. This usually includes what is grown locally. Italian people go to markets often to make sure their ingredients are as fresh as possible. They also only choose fruits and vegetables that are in season.

Eating the Italian Way

Italian people love to eat meals with their families. Traditionally, they return home at midday for several hours to eat their main meal. Large meals include at least three **courses**. Pasta starts the meal. The main course is usually a small portion of meat. A sweet treat completes the meal. Sometimes a small course called *antipasto* is served before the pasta course.

Fashionably Late

At dinner parties, it is often polite to show up a few minutes late. If you show up on time, the host might still be cooking!

In general, Italian people have good table manners. They follow several rules to avoid offending the chef. Italian chefs provide the seasonings they believe should go with the meal. Asking for other ones, such as Parmesan cheese, is considered an insult. Italian people also do not eat bread before the meal. At casual dinners, they dip it in the leftover sauces from the main course. It is considered a compliment to the chef.

Regional Foods

Italian food is popular around the world. However, true Italian cuisine is difficult to define. Most foreign restaurants barely scratch the surface of all that Italy has to offer. Each of the country's 20 regions has unique dishes. These reflect the variety of local ingredients and cultures found in Italian cuisine.

Where is Italy?

Lombardy

panettone:
A sweet dessert bread with raisins and candied fruits inside, served around Christmastime

Sardinia

sebadas:
Deep-fried pastries filled with cheese and drizzled with honey

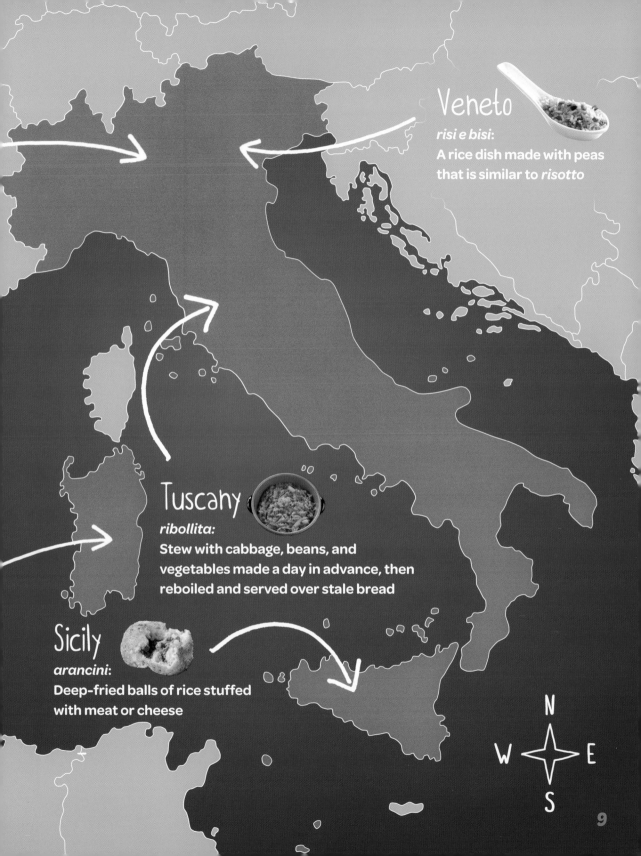

Veneto

risi e bisi:
A rice dish made with peas that is similar to *risotto*

Tuscany

ribollita:
Stew with cabbage, beans, and vegetables made a day in advance, then reboiled and served over stale bread

Sicily

arancini:
Deep-fried balls of rice stuffed with meat or cheese

N
W · E
S

Sweet Treats

Italian children usually only drink water with their meals. They can choose sparkling or plain water. To them, flavored drinks compete with the flavor of the food. For breakfast, they will sometimes drink warm milk. Sodas such as Coca-Cola are a treat and occasionally enjoyed with pizza.

International Hit

Nutella is one sweet Italian creation. This chocolate hazelnut spread has become popular all over Europe and the United States.

gelato

biscotti

tiramisu

cannoli

For dessert, Italian people usually eat simple yet sweet foods. Sometimes, this is just fresh fruit or a scoop of **gelato**. Other times they have coffee with a hard cookie called *biscotti*. Richer desserts include *tiramisu*. This treat features cookies layered with a sweet cheese and dipped in coffee. Italian people also enjoy *cannoli*. These deep-fried pastry tubes are filled with sweet ricotta cheese.

Getting Ready to Cook

Before you begin cooking, read these safety reminders. Make sure you also read the recipes you will follow. You will want to gather all the ingredients and cooking tools right away.

Safety Reminders

 Ask an adult for permission to start cooking. An adult should be near when you use kitchen appliances or a sharp knife.

 Wash your hands with soapy water before you start cooking. Wash your hands again if you lick your fingers or handle raw meat.

 If you have long hair, tie it back. Remove any bracelets or rings that you have on.

 Wear an apron when you cook. It will protect food from dirt and your clothes from spills and splatters.

 Always use oven mitts when handling hot cookware. If you accidentally burn yourself, run the burned area under cold water and tell an adult.

 If a fire starts, call an adult immediately. Never throw water on a fire. Baking soda can smother small flames. A lid can put out a fire in a pot or pan. If flames are large and leaping, call 911 and leave the house.

 Clean up the kitchen when you are done cooking. Make sure all appliances are turned off.

Insalata Caprese

IN-sal-AH-tah ka-PRAY-say

Fresh Italian Salad
Serves 4

Insalata Caprese is often served as an appetizer, side dish, or as a sandwich filling. Its red, white, and green ingredients represent the colors of the Italian flag.

What You'll Need

- 1/4 cup olive oil
- 3 tablespoons balsamic vinegar
- 16 fresh mozzarella balls
- 16 cherry tomatoes
- 16 basil leaves
- dish
- strainer
- toothpicks

Let's Make It!

1

Pour the olive oil in a dish, then sprinkle with the balsamic vinegar.

2

Use a strainer to drain the mozzarella balls.

3

Wrap a basil leaf around a tomato, then pass a toothpick through them.

Enjoy!

Add the mozzarella ball to the toothpick, then set the skewer in the dish. Continue until the plate is filled. Serve cold.

Risotto

ree-ZO-toe

Creamy Italian Rice
Serves 4

Risotto was first made in Milan, but it has become a staple meal throughout all of Italy. It is often prepared with a variety of vegetables, meats, or seafood.

What You'll Need

- 2 1/2 cups chicken stock (substitute: vegetable stock)
- 2 cups water
- 3 tablespoons olive oil
- 1 chopped onion
- salt
- pepper
- 1 cup Arborio rice
- 2 cups peas
- 2 tablespoons butter
- 1/2 cup grated Parmesan cheese
- small saucepan
- medium saucepan
- stirring spoon

Let's Make It!

1

Pour the chicken stock and water into a small saucepan, then bring to a simmer.

2

Add the olive oil to a medium saucepan over medium heat, then add the onion and a pinch of salt and pepper.

3

Add the rice, then stir well. Cook for about 2 minutes.

4

Add half of the broth to the rice, then simmer over low heat for about 6 minutes or until the liquid is absorbed. Continue adding the broth about 1 cup at a time, and allow it to be absorbed before adding more.

5

When the rice is soft and creamy with just a little liquid in the pan, stir in the peas and butter. Cook for 2-3 minutes.

Enjoy!

Cover with Parmesan cheese, then serve hot.

With the Grain

Rice was introduced to Italy by Arab traders in the Middle Ages. Italy is now the leading rice producer in Europe.

Pizza
PEET-za

Flatbread with Toppings
Serves 4

Modern Italian pizzas originated in Naples in the 1700s. City workers added tomatoes to flatbread for a cheap meal.

What You'll Need

- 2 1/2 cups flour
- 1 teaspoon instant yeast
- 1 teaspoon salt
- 3/4 cup water
- 1 tablespoon olive oil
- 1/2 cup pasta sauce
- 1 teaspoon dried basil
- 1 chopped garlic clove
- 2-3 cups mozzarella cheese

- 2 medium bowls
- 2 stirring spoons
- towel
- rolling pin
- 2 baking sheets (substitute: pizza stones)

Let's Make It!

1

Combine the flour, yeast, and salt in a medium bowl, then add the water and olive oil. Stir until the dough is wet and soft.

2

Knead the dough on a flat, floured surface for about 5 minutes. Cover with a towel and let rest.

3

Preheat the oven to 450 degrees Fahrenheit, then combine the pasta sauce, basil, and garlic in a bowl.

4

Knead the dough a bit more, then separate it into two balls. Use a rolling pin to flatten the dough into two 10-inch circles.

5

Transfer the dough onto greased baking sheets. Spread the sauce equally on each pizza.

Enjoy!

Add the cheese and any other desired toppings, then drizzle a little olive oil on the pizzas. Cook in the oven for 10–12 minutes or until crisp. Serve hot.

Old Favorite

Flatbreads served with toppings have been around for thousands of years. They were also enjoyed by the ancient Greeks and Egyptians.

Minestrone
ME-neh-STRO-neh

Hearty Italian Soup
Serves 4

Minestrone is a common soup that has been served in Italy for thousands of years. There are many kinds of minestrone. Ingredients are often leftovers and fresh vegetables.

What You'll Need

- 1 tablespoon olive oil
- 1 large chopped onion
- 3 chopped garlic cloves
- 3 large chopped carrots
- 2 large chopped potatoes
- 2 chopped celery sticks
- 14 ounces chopped tomatoes
- 2 cups vegetable stock
- 2 tablespoons tomato puree

- 15 ounces cannellini beans (substitute: butter beans)
- 1/2 head shredded Savoy cabbage
- water
- 1 cup dried pasta shells
- large pot
- saucepan
- strainer

Let's Make It!

1

Pour 1 tablespoon of olive oil into a large pot over medium heat, then add the onion and garlic. Sauté for 2–3 minutes, then add the carrots, potatoes, and celery. Sauté for another 3–5 minutes.

2

Add the chopped tomatoes, vegetable stock, and tomato puree, then bring to a boil.

3

Add the beans and cabbage, then reduce to low heat. Simmer for at least 40 minutes.

4

Fill a small saucepan about halfway with water, then bring to a boil and add the pasta. Cook until firm, then drain the water.

Enjoy!

When the soup is ready, add the pasta. Cook for 2–3 minutes, then serve hot.

Whatever You've Got

Minestrone is an example of *cucina povera*, which means "cooking of the poor." This style of cooking uses whatever is on hand to make the least amount of food waste.

Glossary

climates—the usual weather conditions in specific areas

courses—different parts of meals served one at a time

cuisine—a style of cooking unique to a certain area or group of people

diversity—a variety of different cultures or landscapes

gelato—Italian ice cream; gelato is creamier and denser than American ice cream.

staples—foods that are widely and regularly used

traditions—customs, ideas, or beliefs that have been passed down from one generation to the next

To Learn More

AT THE LIBRARY

De Laurentiis, Giada. *Naples!* New York, N.Y.: Grosset & Dunlap, 2013.

Harms, Julia. *Recipe and Craft Guide to Italy*. Hockessin, Del.: Mitchell Lane Publishers, 2012.

Simmons, Walter. *Italy*. Minneapolis, Minn.: Bellwether Media, 2011.

ON THE WEB

Learning more about Italy is as easy as 1, 2, 3.

1. Go to www.factsurfer.com.

2. Enter "Italy" into the search box.

3. Click the "Surf" button and you will see a list of related web sites.

With factsurfer.com, finding more information is just a click away.

Index

The images in this book are reproduced through the courtesy of: Shutterstock, front cover; Andrea Leone, title page; Regina Pryanichnikova, credits page; Julian Weber, table of contents; Aleksandra Duda, pp. 4-5; Tim Graham/ Glow Images, p. 5 (left); Olha Afanasieva, p. 5 (left); Exactostock/ SuperStock, p. 6; Wavebreak Media LTD/ Newscom, p. 7; Luiz Rocha, p. 8 (top); marmo81, p. 8 (bottom); Lapina Maria, p. 9 (left); Denio Rigacci, p. 9 (middle); In Tune, p. 9 (right); Rob Hainer, p. 10 (left); Jon Le-Bon, p. 10 (right); Jill Chen, p. 11 (top left); ninette_luz, p. 11 (top right); bestv, p. 11 (bottom left); Isantilli, p. 11 (bottom right); Tomas Rodriguez/ Corbis, p. 12 (left); Henglein and Steets/ Glow Images, p. 12 (right); Jouke van Keulen, p. 13; siro46, p. 14 (bottom); andersphoto, p. 18 (bottom); homydesign, p. 22; all other photos courtesy of bswing.